Mythical Beasts

MYTHICAL CREATURES WITH WINGS

By Joanne Rippin

Cavendish Square

Published in 2023 by Cavendish Square Publishing, LLC
2544 Clinton Street, Buffalo, NY 14224

Originally Published in English by Haynes Publishing under the title: *Mythical Beasts Pocket Manual* © Haynes Publishing 2020

Website: cavendishsq.com

Design and layout by Richard Parsons
Thanks to the following agencies for use of their images:
Alamy; pp 5, 29, 30. **Bridgeman Art Library**. **Getty**. **Shutterstock;** Grom08 (cover).

Cataloging-in-Publication Data

Names: Rippin, Joanne.
Title: Mythical creatures with wings / Joanne Rippin.
Description: New York : Cavendish Square Publishing, 2023. | Series: Mythical beasts | Includes glossary and index.
Identifiers: ISBN 9781502667304 (pbk.) | ISBN 9781502667311 (library bound) | ISBN 9781502667328 (ebook)
Subjects: LCSH: Animals, Mythical--Juvenile literature. | Mythology--Juvenile literature.
Classification: LCC GR825.R577 2023 | DDC 398.24'54--dc23

CPSIA compliance information: Batch #CWCSQ23: For further information contact Cavendish Square Publishing LLC at 1-877-980-4450.

Printed in the United States of America

Find us on

The Author

Joanne is an experienced writer and editor, who has published many historical books on a wide variety of subjects. She has a long-standing fascination with mythical creatures, and has a dog who thinks it's half human.

Contents

CHIMERA

FIRE-BREATHING MONSTER

The Chimera's name means "she-goat." She was a hybrid monster made up of three different animals. She had the head and foreparts of a huge lion, the body of a goat, and the hindquarters of a dragon or snake. Some descriptions say there was a goat's head, too, and that at the end of her tail was a snake's head. Some poets said the heads could breathe fire. In later years, the Chimera was sometimes shown with the wings of a dragon. Although her head has the mane of a male lion, the Chimera is usually referred to as being female.

THE SLAYING OF THE CHIMERA

The Chimera lived in a cave in the kingdom of Lycia, and she destroyed the countryside, burning crops and terrifying the people. The king, Iobates, gave the hero Bellerophon the task of slaying, or killing, it. Even though many men had tried and failed to kill the monster, Bellerophon felt there must be a way to succeed, and he prayed to the goddess Athena to help him. She appeared to him in a dream and told him to catch the winged horse, Pegasus, so that he could attack the Chimera from the air. Bellerophon caught the horse and flew to the Chimera's lair. From above, he threw a lead-tipped spear at the creature, aiming it straight into her fiery mouth. The lead quickly melted, and the Chimera suffocated and died.

·BELLEROPHON·SLAYS·THE·CHIMÆRA·

Did you know?

Another way we still use the word "chimera" is to describe a hope or a dream that is extremely unlikely ever to come true.

Fire-Breathing Landscape

Lycia was a kingdom in Asia Minor, now known as Turkey, where volcanic gas vents are common. At night, it's possible to see these sudden jets of flame appearing from the towns and villages below. Perhaps the myth of a fire-breathing creature came about as an explanation for why these distant mountains would seem to burn after nightfall.

Known Facts

Name:	Chimera
Family status:	Mother was woman-snake Echidna, father was man-dragon Typhon
Career:	Destroying the Lycian countryside
Personality:	Fierce, strong, and destructive
Appearance:	Lion's head, goat's body, dragon's wings, snake tail
Symbolizes:	An impossible dream; extreme danger

Chimera in science

The name chimera has been used in modern medicine to describe an organism with two separate sets of DNA, containing the code to make two different organisms.

Griffin

Noble and Gentle Hybrid

This magnificent creature has a lion's body and the head, wings, and talons of an eagle. The griffin (sometimes spelled "gryphon") was a favorite wall decoration in ancient Mesopotamian and Egyptian art, where it may have been used as a symbol of protection. It was shown either lying down or seated on its hindquarters, and was often paired with the sphinx—a creature with the body of a lion and the head of a human. Like dragons, it is sometimes said to guard treasure.

Characteristics

Since medieval times, the griffin has been thought of as sacred and mostly kind. It is associated with healing, and because it is said to mate for life, it became a symbol of marriage in Christianity. It has often been used as a symbol in heraldry. It is sometimes called the "king of all creatures" because it is the offspring of an eagle (the king of the birds) and a lion (the king of the beasts). The griffin's prey is most often the horse.

Did you know?

The griffin's name comes from the Greek word *gryps*, meaning "curved" or "hooked," which refers to its beak.

ALEXANDER AND GRIFFINS

A legend says that Alexander the Great wanted to see the whole world, so he caught two griffins, harnessed them together with a seat in between, and then held two long sticks with lumps of meat on the ends in front of their beaks to make them fly high into the sky. Other stories about griffins say that one of their feathers will cure blindness and that a cup carved from a griffin claw will change color if the drink inside it is poisoned.

Known Facts

Name:	Griffin
Family status:	Offspring of the king of the birds (eagle) and king of the beasts (lion)
Career:	Guarding people and treasure
Personality:	Gentle, loyal, but fierce if its treasure is stolen
Appearance:	Head, wings, and feet of an eagle, body of a lion
Symbolizes:	Marriage, healing, protection, power

Griffins and treasure

In the legends of Scythia (now part of modern Iran), griffins were said to dig up gold and emeralds from the earth with their talons. They would then use these gems to build nests high up in the mountains.

Hippogriff

Half Horse, Half Griffin

The hippogriff is a relatively modern mythical beast, which only enters into tales and legends in medieval times. It is said to be the offspring of a griffin and a horse. Because these two creatures are meant to be mortal enemies, the hippogriff is associated with true love that overcomes obstacles. Like a griffin, the hippogriff has the head and beak of an eagle, claws with talons, and feathered wings, but the hindquarters, legs, and tail of a horse.

Heroes and Magicians

The hippogriff was a favorite creature in European poems and tales in the Middle Ages. It was probably invented by the Italian author Ludovico Ariosto. In his book *Orlando Furioso,* hippogriffs are ridden by various heroes to rescue maidens. They are said to be able to fly as fast as lightning, and they once carried a knight to the moon and then around the world. In the same book, they were also the chosen mount of the wizard Atlante, who harnessed two of them to a chariot. There is a sculpture showing this on St. Mark's basilica in Venice. Perhaps this link with wizards is what inspired J. K. Rowling.

Hippogriffs in the Wizarding World

In the Harry Potter series, hippogriffs are said to be noble creatures, but proud and extremely dangerous unless tamed. This should only be attempted by a fully trained witch or wizard. They are carnivorous and mostly eat insects, birds, and small mammals such as mice and ferrets. Their coats can come in several colors, including gray, chestnut, and inky black. As Hagrid tells Harry, they care a lot about etiquette and politeness, and if you want to ride one you have to approach with respect, bow, and wait for a response.

In Harry Potter and the Prisoner of Azkaban, *Hagrid tells the class that when approaching a hippogriff, they must maintain eye contact and bow in greeting. If the hippogriff doesn't bow back, they need to retreat very quickly.*

Known Facts

Name:	Hippogriff
Family status:	Offspring of a griffin and a horse
Career:	Ridden by heroes and wizards
Personality:	Noble, proud, and may attack if offended
Appearance:	Head of a griffin, body of a horse; their coats are a combination of feathers and hair
Symbolizes:	True love

Did you know?

The hippogriff's name comes from a combination of the Greek word *hippos*, meaning "horse," and griffin. Ariosto based the animal on a proverb of the time that used the idea of a horse mating with a griffin to represent something impossible.

PEGASUS

MAJESTIC WINGED HORSE

Although he doesn't appear very often in Greek myths, images of Pegasus, a beautiful white winged horse, have been used in stories, paintings, and movies for years. Legends say that Pegasus was the child of Medusa, a Gorgon, and Poseidon, the god of the sea. When Medusa was killed by Perseus, Pegasus and his brother Chrysaor (a human soldier with a gold sword) were born, springing fully formed from Medusa's neck after her head had been severed.

Bellerophon

The story of how Bellerophon caught Pegasus on the advice of Athena, and used him to kill the Chimera, is told on page 4 of this book. Once the Chimera was dead, Bellerophon was so pleased with himself that he decided he deserved to join the gods on Mount Olympus, so he tried to ride Pegasus to the top of the mountain. Before they reached the home of the gods, an outraged Zeus ordered Pegasus to throw Bellerophon from his back. The horse obeyed, and Bellerophon fell to Earth. Amazingly, he survived, but his legs and eyes were ruined for the rest of his life. Later legends in the Middle Ages replace Bellerophon with Perseus as the rider of Pegasus after he killed Medusa.

Did you know?

The name Pegasus comes from the Greek word for water spring, *pegae*. This may be because he was born near the "springs of Ocean," but might also be because he had the ability to create water streams wherever he struck his hoof.

Star Horse

As a reward to Pegasus for his obedience and to thank him for stopping Bellerophon from reaching the home of the gods, Zeus welcomed Pegasus to Mount Olympus. The king of the gods gave Pegasus a place in his personal stables and awarded him with the honor of carrying his thunderbolts. When Pegasus died, Zeus transformed the horse into a constellation.

Known Facts

Name: Pegasus

Family status: Mother was Medusa, father was Poseidon, brother was Chrysaor

Career: Helped Bellerophon kill the Chimera before living on Mount Olympus and carrying Zeus's thunderbolts

Personality: Obedient and courageous

Appearance: Strong and beautiful; white with huge feathered wings

Symbolizes: Speed, beauty, majesty

Waters of inspiration

After he was born, Pegasus flew to Mount Helicon, home of the Muses—the nymphs of creativity. When he arrived, he stamped on the ground and a freshwater spring appeared. This spring was later called the Hippocrene, or "horse spring," and was said to be a source of poetic inspiration.

PHOENIX

FABULOUS, IMMORTAL, FIERY BIRD

Egyptian, Persian, Slavic, Greek, and Roman legends all have versions of the phoenix, although it was the ancient Greeks who gave it this name. There is only one phoenix alive at any time. Some stories say that it lives for 500 years; others say its life span is up to 1,000 years. In most stories, the phoenix is said to live in heaven. It builds a nest in the highest tree and each morning it rises to greet the sun with outspread wings and a beautiful song. In some stories, the bird eats fruit and rare spices, such as frankincense.

FIERY BIRD

The phoenix is as large as an eagle but has brilliant red and gold feathers, a shining beak, and sapphire eyes. As the years pass, its brilliant feathers gradually fade, and when the bird feels the end of its life approaching, it gathers cinnamon and other spices and carries them to Phoenicia (modern-day Lebanon), where it builds its own pyre. The next morning, when the sun rises, the phoenix sings the most beautiful song in the world. After it finishes, the pyre bursts into flames and burns the bird to ashes with it. All that is left is a tiny worm. Three days later, this worm takes on the form of a bird and a new phoenix rises from the ashes. The young bird carries the ashes to the ancient Egyptian city of Heliopolis ("City of the Sun") before returning to its home in heaven. In some stories, the phoenix dies in Heliopolis rather than traveling there after its rebirth.

Did you know?

Chinese, Indian, and ancient Jewish traditions also tell stories of a mythical bird that bursts into flames at the end of its life and then regenerates. The Japanese phoenix—the Ho-o or sun bird—was adopted as a symbol of the imperial household.

Immortality and Healing

Ancient Egyptians associated the phoenix with immortality—living forever. The Romans later linked this to Rome, which they thought of as the "undying city." Because of its ability to be reborn, early Christians used the phoenix as a symbol of life after death. In later years, people added healing powers to the myth of the phoenix. The feathers or tears of the phoenix were said to be able to cure illness and disease. For example, in some versions of the role-playing game Dungeons and Dragons, players can use these items to heal any wounds they have.

Known Facts

Name:	Phoenix
Family status:	There is only one phoenix; as a regenerating creature, it is its own parent and offspring
Career:	Lives in heaven, greets the sun with its song
Personality:	Clever, wise, and gentle; later with healing powers
Appearance:	Magnificent red and gold feathers with a long tail
Symbolizes:	Rebirth, renewal, transformation

Phoenix, Arizona

Between AD 700 and 1400, an advanced civilization stood in what is now Arizona. When white people moved into the area, they called the town Phoenix because it rose from the ashes of this past city.

Roc

Fierce and Gigantic Bird

A roc is so huge that its wingspan measures 48 feet (15 m). In flight, its shadow darkens the ground below. Some traditions say the bird is white, while others say it looks similar to an eagle, with red-brown feathers. All legends agree that the bird is huge and in appearance is similar to an eagle or a vulture.

Sinbad the Sailor

Sinbad was the hero of many Arabian tales. In one story, Sinbad was marooned on a remote desert island. To escape, he tied himself to the leg of a nesting roc, and when the giant bird took off in search of food, Sinbad rode on its huge talon. On another voyage, Sinbad and his shipmates ate roc eggs for food and were then chased down by the furious parents, who dropped boulders onto their ship.

Sinbad

Did you know?

The fossilized eggs of the extinct flightless bird Aepyornis helped fuel the legend of the roc.

Fact or Fiction?

The roc (sometimes spelled rukh) is known in folktales from Madagascar to the China Seas. Sailors said it could carry a ship in its beak. The Madagascan roc's common prey is the elephant, which it can lift in its enormous claws and carry off with ease. Stories of the roc may be based on the garuda—a birdlike creature in Hindu myths that preyed on elephants and giant snakes. Like the kraken and the unicorn, this is a mythical creature that people believed really existed. The explorer Marco Polo wrote that Kublai Khan, ruler of China in the 13th century, owned a feather that he believed came from a roc. Some historians believe it was actually a leaf from the raffia palm.

Known Facts

Name: Roc or rukh

Family status: A giant bird of prey; may have been inspired by now-extinct creatures

Career: Hunting elephants, frightening sailors, protecting their chicks

Personality: Fierce, very strong, good parents

Appearance: Like a huge eagle or vulture

Symbols: Elephants, giant feathers

Haast's eagle

Until about AD 1500, a giant bird similar to the roc lived in New Zealand. It was called Haast's eagle, and its wingspan was about 10 feet (3 m) long. It was big enough to prey on moas—flightless birds similar to ostriches—and may have even hunted humans.

SIMURGH

PERSIAN BIRD OF WISDOM

The earliest mention of the Simurgh is found in the *Avesta,* a holy book of the Zoroastrian religion. Zoroastrianism is one of the world's oldest religions; in fact, it may be up to 4,000 years old. The Simurgh herself is said to be so old that she has seen the destruction of the world three times over. This has given her so much wisdom and learning that she possesses the knowledge of all the ages.

Heavenly Bird of Healing

The Simurgh is sometimes described as a peacock with multicolored feathers, the head of a dog, and a lion's claws. In Persian art, however, it is more often painted as a giant bird similar to a phoenix. The Simurgh is said to live in the Hōm, or the Tree of Life. This tree represented the union of Earth and the heavens, and the Simurgh served as a messenger between the two. The Hōm is said to contain powerful medicine that can heal all illnesses, so when the Simurgh takes off or lands from there, her wings make the seeds fly around the world, taking their healing powers to all corners of the globe. A feather from the Simurgh will also cure all diseases.

Did you know?

The Simurgh is on the coat of arms of Uzbekistan. The Afghan football team, Simorgh Alborz FC, is named after her.

THE SIMURGH AND PRINCE ZAAL

The most famous story of the Simurgh is her adoption of an abandoned baby, Zaal, the albino son of King Saam. Saam had abandoned the baby on the mountainside because he believed Zaal's white hair was a sign of bad luck. The Simurgh heard the baby's cries, rescued him, and raised him until he was grown up, loving him as if he was her own. When Prince Zaal returned to human society, the Simurgh gave him a few of her feathers, which he was to burn if he ever needed her help. A few years later, Zaal's wife was giving birth to their first child, but there were complications and it seemed as if both mother and child would not survive, so Zaal burned one of the feathers. The Simurgh appeared and helped the prince safely remove the baby from his mother's womb, saving both of them and successfully performing history's first caesarean section (often called a c-section today).

The Simurgh rescues the baby, Prince Zaal, and carries him back to her nest.

Known Facts

Name:	Simurgh, also spelled Simorgh and Simurg
Family status:	There is only one Simurgh, and she is thousands of years old
Career:	Knowing everything there is to know, linking Earth with heaven, healing
Personality:	Kind, nurturing, clever
Appearance:	Sometimes described as a hybrid creature with wings; more often shown as a huge, beautiful bird with a peacock-like tail
Symbolizes:	Medical care, holiness, royalty

Fiery bird

Sometimes compared to the phoenix, the Simurgh is said in some accounts to live until she is 1,700 years old, when she plunges into flames and is born again.

Glossary

basilica: A Roman Catholic church where a bishop sits.

etiquette: The rules governing the proper way to behave or to do something.

heraldry: The practice of tracing and recording family history and creating coats of arms

marooned: Abandoned in a place that is difficult to escape from.

proverb: A short, well-known saying containing a wise thought.

pyre: A heap of wood for burning a dead body.

suffocate: To die due to lack of air.

For More Information

Sharma, Bulbul, and Upamanyu Bhattacharyya. *Fantastic Creatures in Mythology.* Gurgaon, Haryana, India: Penguin Random House India, 2021

MysticBeasts: *https://mysticbeasts.com/flying-mythical-creatures/*

Index